NAME:

COMPANY:

ID:

BASE:

| Date: | Registration: |
| Show time: | A/C type: |

Route:	Flight no:
Duration:	Passengers:
Scheduled departure:	Scheduled arrival:
Actual departure:	Actual arrival:

| Layover info: | Notes: |

| Date: | Registration: |
| Show time: | A/C type: |

Route:	Flight no:
Duration:	Passengers:
Scheduled departure:	Scheduled arrival:
Actual departure:	Actual arrival:

| Layover info: | Notes: |

Date:　　　　　　　Registration:
　　　Show time:　　　　　　A/C type:

Route:　　　　　　　　Flight no:
Duration:　　　　　　　Passengers:
Scheduled departure:　Scheduled arrival:
Actual departure:　　　Actual arrival:

Layover info:　　　　　Notes:

Date:　　　　　　　Registration:
　　　Show time:　　　　　　A/C type:

Route:　　　　　　　　Flight no:
Duration:　　　　　　　Passengers:
Scheduled departure:　Scheduled arrival:
Actual departure:　　　Actual arrival:

Layover info:　　　　　Notes:

Date: Registration:
        Show time: A/C type:

Route: Flight no:
Duration: Passengers:
Scheduled departure: Scheduled arrival:
Actual departure: Actual arrival:

Layover info: Notes:

---∽---

Date: Registration:
        Show time: A/C type:

Route: Flight no:
Duration: Passengers:
Scheduled departure: Scheduled arrival:
Actual departure: Actual arrival:

Layover info: Notes:

Date: Registration:
 Show time: A/C type:

Route: Flight no:
Duration: Passengers:
Scheduled departure: Scheduled arrival:
Actual departure: Actual arrival:

Layover info:

Notes:

Date: Registration:
 Show time: A/C type:

Route: Flight no:
Duration: Passengers:
Scheduled departure: Scheduled arrival:
Actual departure: Actual arrival:

Layover info:

Notes:

Date: Registration:
      Show time: A/C type:

Route: Flight no:
Duration: Passengers:
Scheduled departure: Scheduled arrival:
Actual departure: Actual arrival:

Layover info: Notes:

Date: Registration:
      Show time: A/C type:

Route: Flight no:
Duration: Passengers:
Scheduled departure: Scheduled arrival:
Actual departure: Actual arrival:

Layover info: Notes:

Date: Registration:
Show time: A/C type:

Route: Flight no:
Duration: Passengers:
Scheduled departure: Scheduled arrival:
Actual departure: Actual arrival:

Layover info:

Notes:

Date: Registration:
Show time: A/C type:

Route: Flight no:
Duration: Passengers:
Scheduled departure: Scheduled arrival:
Actual departure: Actual arrival:

Layover info:

Notes:

Date: Registration:
Show time: A/C type:

Route: Flight no:
Duration: Passengers:
Scheduled departure: Scheduled arrival:
Actual departure: Actual arrival:

Layover info:

Notes:

Date: Registration:
Show time: A/C type:

Route: Flight no:
Duration: Passengers:
Scheduled departure: Scheduled arrival:
Actual departure: Actual arrival:

Layover info:

Notes:

Date: Registration:
Show time: A/C type:

Route: Flight no:
Duration: Passengers:
Scheduled departure: Scheduled arrival:
Actual departure: Actual arrival:

Layover info:

Notes:

Date: Registration:
Show time: A/C type:

Route: Flight no:
Duration: Passengers:
Scheduled departure: Scheduled arrival:
Actual departure: Actual arrival:

Layover info:

Notes:

Date: Registration:
Show time: A/C type:

Route: Flight no:
Duration: Passengers:
Scheduled departure: Scheduled arrival:
Actual departure: Actual arrival:

Layover info: Notes:

Date: Registration:
Show time: A/C type:

Route: Flight no:
Duration: Passengers:
Scheduled departure: Scheduled arrival:
Actual departure: Actual arrival:

Layover info: Notes:

Date: Registration:
Show time: A/C type:

Route: Flight no:
Duration: Passengers:
Scheduled departure: Scheduled arrival:
Actual departure: Actual arrival:

Layover info:

Notes:

Date: Registration:
Show time: A/C type:

Route: Flight no:
Duration: Passengers:
Scheduled departure: Scheduled arrival:
Actual departure: Actual arrival:

Layover info:

Notes:

Date: Registration:
        Show time: A/C type:

Route: Flight no:
Duration: Passengers:
Scheduled departure: Scheduled arrival:
Actual departure: Actual arrival:

Layover info: Notes:

Date: Registration:
        Show time: A/C type:

Route: Flight no:
Duration: Passengers:
Scheduled departure: Scheduled arrival:
Actual departure: Actual arrival:

Layover info: Notes:

Date: Registration:
Show time: A/C type:

Route: Flight no:
Duration: Passengers:
Scheduled departure: Scheduled arrival:
Actual departure: Actual arrival:

Layover info:

Notes:

Date: Registration:
Show time: A/C type:

Route: Flight no:
Duration: Passengers:
Scheduled departure: Scheduled arrival:
Actual departure: Actual arrival:

Layover info:

Notes:

Date: Registration:
Show time: A/C type:

Route: Flight no:
Duration: Passengers:
Scheduled departure: Scheduled arrival:
Actual departure: Actual arrival:

Layover info:

Notes:

Date: Registration:
Show time: A/C type:

Route: Flight no:
Duration: Passengers:
Scheduled departure: Scheduled arrival:
Actual departure: Actual arrival:

Layover info:

Notes:

Date:	Registration:
Show time:	A/C type:

Route:	Flight no:
Duration:	Passengers:
Scheduled departure:	Scheduled arrival:
Actual departure:	Actual arrival:

Layover info:	Notes:

Date:	Registration:
Show time:	A/C type:

Route:	Flight no:
Duration:	Passengers:
Scheduled departure:	Scheduled arrival:
Actual departure:	Actual arrival:

Layover info:	Notes:

Date:	Registration:
Show time:	A/C type:

Route:	Flight no:
Duration:	Passengers:
Scheduled departure:	Scheduled arrival:
Actual departure:	Actual arrival:

Layover info:

Notes:

Date:	Registration:
Show time:	A/C type:

Route:	Flight no:
Duration:	Passengers:
Scheduled departure:	Scheduled arrival:
Actual departure:	Actual arrival:

Layover info:

Notes:

Date:	Registration:
Show time:	A/C type:

Route:	Flight no:
Duration:	Passengers:
Scheduled departure:	Scheduled arrival:
Actual departure:	Actual arrival:

Layover info:	Notes:

Date:	Registration:
Show time:	A/C type:

Route:	Flight no:
Duration:	Passengers:
Scheduled departure:	Scheduled arrival:
Actual departure:	Actual arrival:

Layover info:	Notes:

Date: Registration:
        Show time: A/C type:

Route: Flight no:
Duration: Passengers:
Scheduled departure: Scheduled arrival:
Actual departure: Actual arrival:

Layover info: Notes:

Date: Registration:
        Show time: A/C type:

Route: Flight no:
Duration: Passengers:
Scheduled departure: Scheduled arrival:
Actual departure: Actual arrival:

Layover info: Notes:

Date: Registration:
        Show time: A/C type:

Route: Flight no:
Duration: Passengers:
Scheduled departure: Scheduled arrival:
Actual departure: Actual arrival:

Layover info: Notes:

Date: Registration:
        Show time: A/C type:

Route: Flight no:
Duration: Passengers:
Scheduled departure: Scheduled arrival:
Actual departure: Actual arrival:

Layover info: Notes:

Date:　　　　　　　　Registration:
　　　Show time:　　　　　　　A/C type:

Route:　　　　　　　　Flight no:
Duration:　　　　　　　Passengers:
Scheduled departure:　　Scheduled arrival:
Actual departure:　　　Actual arrival:

Layover info:　　　　　Notes:

Date:　　　　　　　　Registration:
　　　Show time:　　　　　　　A/C type:

Route:　　　　　　　　Flight no:
Duration:　　　　　　　Passengers:
Scheduled departure:　　Scheduled arrival:
Actual departure:　　　Actual arrival:

Layover info:　　　　　Notes:

Date:	Registration:
Show time:	A/C type:

Route:	Flight no:
Duration:	Passengers:
Scheduled departure:	Scheduled arrival:
Actual departure:	Actual arrival:

Layover info:	Notes:

Date:	Registration:
Show time:	A/C type:

Route:	Flight no:
Duration:	Passengers:
Scheduled departure:	Scheduled arrival:
Actual departure:	Actual arrival:

Layover info:	Notes:

Date: Registration:
Show time: A/C type:

Route: Flight no:
Duration: Passengers:
Scheduled departure: Scheduled arrival:
Actual departure: Actual arrival:

Layover info: Notes:

Date: Registration:
Show time: A/C type:

Route: Flight no:
Duration: Passengers:
Scheduled departure: Scheduled arrival:
Actual departure: Actual arrival:

Layover info: Notes:

Date: Registration:
Show time: A/C type:

Route: Flight no:
Duration: Passengers:
Scheduled departure: Scheduled arrival:
Actual departure: Actual arrival:

Layover info:

Notes:

Date: Registration:
Show time: A/C type:

Route: Flight no:
Duration: Passengers:
Scheduled departure: Scheduled arrival:
Actual departure: Actual arrival:

Layover info:

Notes:

Date: Registration:
      Show time: A/C type:

Route: Flight no:
Duration: Passengers:
Scheduled departure: Scheduled arrival:
Actual departure: Actual arrival:

Layover info: Notes:

Date: Registration:
      Show time: A/C type:

Route: Flight no:
Duration: Passengers:
Scheduled departure: Scheduled arrival:
Actual departure: Actual arrival:

Layover info: Notes:

Date:	Registration:
Show time:	A/C type:

Route:	Flight no:
Duration:	Passengers:
Scheduled departure:	Scheduled arrival:
Actual departure:	Actual arrival:

Layover info:	Notes:

Date:	Registration:
Show time:	A/C type:

Route:	Flight no:
Duration:	Passengers:
Scheduled departure:	Scheduled arrival:
Actual departure:	Actual arrival:

Layover info:	Notes:

Date: Registration:
     Show time: A/C type:

Route: Flight no:
Duration: Passengers:
Scheduled departure: Scheduled arrival:
Actual departure: Actual arrival:

Layover info: Notes:

Date: Registration:
     Show time: A/C type:

Route: Flight no:
Duration: Passengers:
Scheduled departure: Scheduled arrival:
Actual departure: Actual arrival:

Layover info: Notes:

Date: Registration:
   Show time: A/C type:

Route: Flight no:
Duration: Passengers:
Scheduled departure: Scheduled arrival:
Actual departure: Actual arrival:

Layover info:

Notes:

Date: Registration:
   Show time: A/C type:

Route: Flight no:
Duration: Passengers:
Scheduled departure: Scheduled arrival:
Actual departure: Actual arrival:

Layover info:

Notes:

Date:	Registration:
Show time:	A/C type:

Route:	Flight no:
Duration:	Passengers:
Scheduled departure:	Scheduled arrival:
Actual departure:	Actual arrival:

Layover info:	Notes:

Date:	Registration:
Show time:	A/C type:

Route:	Flight no:
Duration:	Passengers:
Scheduled departure:	Scheduled arrival:
Actual departure:	Actual arrival:

Layover info:	Notes:

Date:	Registration:
Show time:	A/C type:

Route:	Flight no:
Duration:	Passengers:
Scheduled departure:	Scheduled arrival:
Actual departure:	Actual arrival:

Layover info:	Notes:

Date:	Registration:
Show time:	A/C type:

Route:	Flight no:
Duration:	Passengers:
Scheduled departure:	Scheduled arrival:
Actual departure:	Actual arrival:

Layover info:	Notes:

Date:	Registration:
Show time:	A/C type:

Route:	Flight no:
Duration:	Passengers:
Scheduled departure:	Scheduled arrival:
Actual departure:	Actual arrival:

Layover info:	Notes:

Date:	Registration:
Show time:	A/C type:

Route:	Flight no:
Duration:	Passengers:
Scheduled departure:	Scheduled arrival:
Actual departure:	Actual arrival:

Layover info:	Notes:

Date: Registration:
Show time: A/C type:

Route: Flight no:
Duration: Passengers:
Scheduled departure: Scheduled arrival:
Actual departure: Actual arrival:

Layover info:

Notes:

Date: Registration:
Show time: A/C type:

Route: Flight no:
Duration: Passengers:
Scheduled departure: Scheduled arrival:
Actual departure: Actual arrival:

Layover info:

Notes:

Date:	Registration:
Show time:	A/C type:

Route:	Flight no:
Duration:	Passengers:
Scheduled departure:	Scheduled arrival:
Actual departure:	Actual arrival:

Layover info:	Notes:

Date:	Registration:
Show time:	A/C type:

Route:	Flight no:
Duration:	Passengers:
Scheduled departure:	Scheduled arrival:
Actual departure:	Actual arrival:

Layover info:	Notes:

Date: Registration:
Show time: A/C type:

Route: Flight no:
Duration: Passengers:
Scheduled departure: Scheduled arrival:
Actual departure: Actual arrival:

Layover info:

Notes:

Date: Registration:
Show time: A/C type:

Route: Flight no:
Duration: Passengers:
Scheduled departure: Scheduled arrival:
Actual departure: Actual arrival:

Layover info:

Notes:

Date: Registration:
        Show time: A/C type:

Route: Flight no:
Duration: Passengers:
Scheduled departure: Scheduled arrival:
Actual departure: Actual arrival:

Layover info: Notes:

Date: Registration:
        Show time: A/C type:

Route: Flight no:
Duration: Passengers:
Scheduled departure: Scheduled arrival:
Actual departure: Actual arrival:

Layover info: Notes:

Date: Registration:
Show time: A/C type:

Route: Flight no:
Duration: Passengers:
Scheduled departure: Scheduled arrival:
Actual departure: Actual arrival:

Layover info:

Notes:

Date: Registration:
Show time: A/C type:

Route: Flight no:
Duration: Passengers:
Scheduled departure: Scheduled arrival:
Actual departure: Actual arrival:

Layover info:

Notes:

Date: Registration:
    Show time: A/C type:

Route: Flight no:
Duration: Passengers:
Scheduled departure: Scheduled arrival:
Actual departure: Actual arrival:

Layover info: Notes:

Date: Registration:
    Show time: A/C type:

Route: Flight no:
Duration: Passengers:
Scheduled departure: Scheduled arrival:
Actual departure: Actual arrival:

Layover info: Notes:

Date:	Registration:
Show time:	A/C type:

Route:	Flight no:
Duration:	Passengers:
Scheduled departure:	Scheduled arrival:
Actual departure:	Actual arrival:

Layover info:	Notes:

Date:	Registration:
Show time:	A/C type:

Route:	Flight no:
Duration:	Passengers:
Scheduled departure:	Scheduled arrival:
Actual departure:	Actual arrival:

Layover info:	Notes:

Date: Registration:
    Show time: A/C type:

Route: Flight no:
Duration: Passengers:
Scheduled departure: Scheduled arrival:
Actual departure: Actual arrival:

Layover info: Notes:

Date: Registration:
    Show time: A/C type:

Route: Flight no:
Duration: Passengers:
Scheduled departure: Scheduled arrival:
Actual departure: Actual arrival:

Layover info: Notes:

Date: Registration:
    Show time: A/C type:

Route: Flight no:
Duration: Passengers:
Scheduled departure: Scheduled arrival:
Actual departure: Actual arrival:

Layover info: Notes:

Date: Registration:
    Show time: A/C type:

Route: Flight no:
Duration: Passengers:
Scheduled departure: Scheduled arrival:
Actual departure: Actual arrival:

Layover info: Notes:

Date: Registration:
Show time: A/C type:

Route: Flight no:
Duration: Passengers:
Scheduled departure: Scheduled arrival:
Actual departure: Actual arrival:

Layover info:

Notes:

Date: Registration:
Show time: A/C type:

Route: Flight no:
Duration: Passengers:
Scheduled departure: Scheduled arrival:
Actual departure: Actual arrival:

Layover info:

Notes:

Date: Registration:
Show time: A/C type:

Route: Flight no:
Duration: Passengers:
Scheduled departure: Scheduled arrival:
Actual departure: Actual arrival:

Layover info:

Notes:

Date: Registration:
Show time: A/C type:

Route: Flight no:
Duration: Passengers:
Scheduled departure: Scheduled arrival:
Actual departure: Actual arrival:

Layover info:

Notes:

Date: Registration:
       Show time: A/C type:

Route: Flight no:
Duration: Passengers:
Scheduled departure: Scheduled arrival:
Actual departure: Actual arrival:

Layover info: Notes:

Date: Registration:
       Show time: A/C type:

Route: Flight no:
Duration: Passengers:
Scheduled departure: Scheduled arrival:
Actual departure: Actual arrival:

Layover info: Notes:

Date: Registration:
        Show time: A/C type:

Route: Flight no:
Duration: Passengers:
Scheduled departure: Scheduled arrival:
Actual departure: Actual arrival:

Layover info: Notes:

Date: Registration:
        Show time: A/C type:

Route: Flight no:
Duration: Passengers:
Scheduled departure: Scheduled arrival:
Actual departure: Actual arrival:

Layover info: Notes:

Date: Registration:
    Show time: A/C type:

Route: Flight no:
Duration: Passengers:
Scheduled departure: Scheduled arrival:
Actual departure: Actual arrival:

Layover info: Notes:

Date: Registration:
    Show time: A/C type:

Route: Flight no:
Duration: Passengers:
Scheduled departure: Scheduled arrival:
Actual departure: Actual arrival:

Layover info: Notes:

Date: Registration:
        Show time: A/C type:

Route: Flight no:
Duration: Passengers:
Scheduled departure: Scheduled arrival:
Actual departure: Actual arrival:

Layover info: Notes:

---∞---

Date: Registration:
        Show time: A/C type:

Route: Flight no:
Duration: Passengers:
Scheduled departure: Scheduled arrival:
Actual departure: Actual arrival:

Layover info: Notes:

Date: Registration:
    Show time: A/C type:

Route: Flight no:
Duration: Passengers:
Scheduled departure: Scheduled arrival:
Actual departure: Actual arrival:

Layover info: Notes:

Date: Registration:
    Show time: A/C type:

Route: Flight no:
Duration: Passengers:
Scheduled departure: Scheduled arrival:
Actual departure: Actual arrival:

Layover info: Notes:

Date: Registration:
         Show time: A/C type:

Route: Flight no:
Duration: Passengers:
Scheduled departure: Scheduled arrival:
Actual departure: Actual arrival:

Layover info: Notes:

---∽---

Date: Registration:
         Show time: A/C type:

Route: Flight no:
Duration: Passengers:
Scheduled departure: Scheduled arrival:
Actual departure: Actual arrival:

Layover info: Notes:

Date: Registration:
      Show time: A/C type:

Route: Flight no:
Duration: Passengers:
Scheduled departure: Scheduled arrival:
Actual departure: Actual arrival:

Layover info: Notes:

Date: Registration:
      Show time: A/C type:

Route: Flight no:
Duration: Passengers:
Scheduled departure: Scheduled arrival:
Actual departure: Actual arrival:

Layover info: Notes:

Date:	Registration:
Show time:	A/C type:

Route:	Flight no:
Duration:	Passengers:
Scheduled departure:	Scheduled arrival:
Actual departure:	Actual arrival:

Layover info:	Notes:

Date:	Registration:
Show time:	A/C type:

Route:	Flight no:
Duration:	Passengers:
Scheduled departure:	Scheduled arrival:
Actual departure:	Actual arrival:

Layover info:	Notes:

Date: Registration:
        Show time: A/C type:

Route: Flight no:
Duration: Passengers:
Scheduled departure: Scheduled arrival:
Actual departure: Actual arrival:

Layover info: Notes:

Date: Registration:
        Show time: A/C type:

Route: Flight no:
Duration: Passengers:
Scheduled departure: Scheduled arrival:
Actual departure: Actual arrival:

Layover info: Notes:

Date: Registration:
     Show time: A/C type:

Route: Flight no:
Duration: Passengers:
Scheduled departure: Scheduled arrival:
Actual departure: Actual arrival:

Layover info: Notes:

Date: Registration:
     Show time: A/C type:

Route: Flight no:
Duration: Passengers:
Scheduled departure: Scheduled arrival:
Actual departure: Actual arrival:

Layover info: Notes:

Date: Registration:
        Show time: A/C type:

Route: Flight no:
Duration: Passengers:
Scheduled departure: Scheduled arrival:
Actual departure: Actual arrival:

Layover info: Notes:

Date: Registration:
        Show time: A/C type:

Route: Flight no:
Duration: Passengers:
Scheduled departure: Scheduled arrival:
Actual departure: Actual arrival:

Layover info: Notes:

Date: Registration:
    Show time: A/C type:

Route: Flight no:
Duration: Passengers:
Scheduled departure: Scheduled arrival:
Actual departure: Actual arrival:

Layover info: Notes:

Date: Registration:
    Show time: A/C type:

Route: Flight no:
Duration: Passengers:
Scheduled departure: Scheduled arrival:
Actual departure: Actual arrival:

Layover info: Notes:

Date: Registration:
   Show time: A/C type:

Route: Flight no:
Duration: Passengers:
Scheduled departure: Scheduled arrival:
Actual departure: Actual arrival:

Layover info: Notes:

Date: Registration:
   Show time: A/C type:

Route: Flight no:
Duration: Passengers:
Scheduled departure: Scheduled arrival:
Actual departure: Actual arrival:

Layover info: Notes:

Date: Registration:
     Show time: A/C type:

Route: Flight no:
Duration: Passengers:
Scheduled departure: Scheduled arrival:
Actual departure: Actual arrival:

Layover info: Notes:

Date: Registration:
     Show time: A/C type:

Route: Flight no:
Duration: Passengers:
Scheduled departure: Scheduled arrival:
Actual departure: Actual arrival:

Layover info: Notes:

Date: Registration:
     Show time: A/C type:

Route: Flight no:
Duration: Passengers:
Scheduled departure: Scheduled arrival:
Actual departure: Actual arrival:

Layover info: Notes:

Date: Registration:
     Show time: A/C type:

Route: Flight no:
Duration: Passengers:
Scheduled departure: Scheduled arrival:
Actual departure: Actual arrival:

Layover info: Notes:

Date: Registration:
   Show time: A/C type:

Route: Flight no:
Duration: Passengers:
Scheduled departure: Scheduled arrival:
Actual departure: Actual arrival:

Layover info:

Notes:

Date: Registration:
   Show time: A/C type:

Route: Flight no:
Duration: Passengers:
Scheduled departure: Scheduled arrival:
Actual departure: Actual arrival:

Layover info:

Notes:

Date: Registration:
Show time: A/C type:

Route: Flight no:
Duration: Passengers:
Scheduled departure: Scheduled arrival:
Actual departure: Actual arrival:

Layover info:

Notes:

Date: Registration:
Show time: A/C type:

Route: Flight no:
Duration: Passengers:
Scheduled departure: Scheduled arrival:
Actual departure: Actual arrival:

Layover info:

Notes:

Date: Registration:
      Show time: A/C type:

Route: Flight no:
Duration: Passengers:
Scheduled departure: Scheduled arrival:
Actual departure: Actual arrival:

Layover info: Notes:

Date: Registration:
      Show time: A/C type:

Route: Flight no:
Duration: Passengers:
Scheduled departure: Scheduled arrival:
Actual departure: Actual arrival:

Layover info: Notes:

Date:	Registration:
Show time:	A/C type:

Route:	Flight no:
Duration:	Passengers:
Scheduled departure:	Scheduled arrival:
Actual departure:	Actual arrival:

Layover info:	Notes:

---·∞·---

Date:	Registration:
Show time:	A/C type:

Route:	Flight no:
Duration:	Passengers:
Scheduled departure:	Scheduled arrival:
Actual departure:	Actual arrival:

Layover info:	Notes:

Date: Registration:
    Show time: A/C type:

Route: Flight no:
Duration: Passengers:
Scheduled departure: Scheduled arrival:
Actual departure: Actual arrival:

Layover info: Notes:

Date: Registration:
    Show time: A/C type:

Route: Flight no:
Duration: Passengers:
Scheduled departure: Scheduled arrival:
Actual departure: Actual arrival:

Layover info: Notes:

UNITS OF MEASUREMENT

Measurement	Calculation	Result
Knots	Multiply by 1.85	Kilometres per hour
Knots	Multiply by 1.15	Miles per hour
Feet	Divide by 3.28	Metres
Miles	Multiply by 1.61	Kilometres
Miles	Divide by 1.15	Nautical miles
Nautical miles	Multiply by 1.85	Kilometres
Celsius	Multiply by 1.8, add 32	Fahrenheit
Fahrenheit	Subtract 32 , divide by 1.8	Celsius
Kilograms	Multiply by 2.2	Pounds
Centimetres	Divide by 2.54	Inches
Pounds per square inch	Divide by 14.5	Bars

Category	Unit of measurement	Abbreviation
Speed	Knots	kn
Vertical speed	Feet per minute	ft/min
Horizontal distance	Nautical miles	nm
	Kilometres	km
Vertical distance	Feet	ft
	Metres	m
Temperature and dew point	Centigrade	°C
	Fahrenheit	°F
Air pressure	Millibars	hpa
	Hecto pascals	mb
	Inches of mercury	In.Hg
Mass	Kilogram	kg
	Pounds	lbs

Printed in Great Britain
by Amazon